VIOLENCE PREVENTION

WE ALL CAN HELP

JOHN FREAS

NEWMAN SPRINGS PUBLISHING
320 Broad Street
Red Bank, NJ 07701

First originally published by Newman Springs Publishing 2023

ISBN 979-8-89061-016-4 (Paperback)
ISBN 979-8-89061-017-1 (Digital)

Printed in the United States of America

CONTENTS

———

PREFACE

———

Each day in the news, we hear about people being killed or wounded. These reports include gang violence, sexual violence, child abuse, terrorism, riots, international conflicts, domestic violence, mass shootings, police actions, and suicides. These tragedies do not have to happen. There are ways to prevent them. The purpose of this book is to describe the causes of violence and to show the variety of ways each of us can help to make this world a safer place in which to live.

When policymakers respond to mass shootings or other forms of gun violence, they seem to focus on controlling access to firearms, improving mental health, or fortifying schools. There is a place for these changes, but this book demonstrates that violence prevention requires a much broader view of the factors causing violence. These factors include the way parents teach values to their children, the skills needed to resolve conflicts peacefully, the things each of us can do to help children learn to respect all people, and the things schools and community organizations can do to reinforce these values and skills.

Most books on violence prevention focus on specific types of violence, and many are designed for a scholarly audience. This book uses language that is easy to understand, and it is short enough to be read quickly. It also shows how the same prevention strategies relate to all types of violence. Hopefully, it can be used to facilitate discussion and create involvement in violence prevention activities by local, state, and national policymakers, religious groups, civic organizations, and concerned citizens.

The research was informed by the author's professional career working to resolve social problems and his twenty years of part-time study of the topic after retirement. This study included reading numerous books, searching the Internet, and discussing the issues with several different people.

INTRODUCTION

———

Each year, violence results in a huge amount of suffering and death and economic cost. The cost of violence around the world has been estimated at $14 trillion per year. This is $1,853 for every person alive according to research by the Institute for Economics and Peace. This includes direct and indirect costs of $8.3 trillion and $5.7 trillion for lost opportunity costs.[1] Direct costs include things like medical care, policing, litigation, and incarceration. Indirect costs include long-term effects on the victim and perpetrator such as lost wages, psychological effects, pain, and suffering. Lost opportunity costs include things like lifetime earnings lost by the deceased.[2]

When a person or a nation chooses to resort to violence, that choice may be a split-second decision or the result of long deliberation, but usually, a nonviolent choice could have been made instead. In this book, we will show that frequently, the nonviolent choice would have been less expensive in lives and money and more effective for long-term results.

Notes

[1] Dominic Dudley, "Cost of Violence around the World Estimated at $14 Trillion a Year with U.S. Facing Biggest Bill," *Forbes*, June 12, 2019, https://www.forbes.com/sites/dominicdudley/2019/cost-of-violence.

[2] NIH National Library of Medicine, "6 Direct and Indirect Costs of Violence," Viewed December 30, 2022, ncbi.nlm.nih.gov/books/NBK189992/.

Three different factors can set the stage for violence to occur. When violence happens, it usually involves two or more of these factors.

1. A person is predisposed to violence or is limited in the ability to control violent impulses.
2. A person experiences something that triggers a violent response.
3. Two or more people are experiencing a conflict, and they fail to resolve it peacefully.

Prevention strategies can be designed in relation to each of these three factors, and each interested person can find ways to take part in preventing violence by matching their interests and abilities with one or more of these strategies.

Whether we are looking at personal violence or terrorism or international conflicts, the same prevention strategies can apply.

- Help people learn the importance of respecting all people regardless of race, ethnicity, religion, disability, income, or sexual orientation. A lot of violence is caused by people being disrespected for one reason or another.
- Promote equal opportunities for all people. A lot of terrorism and international disputes are based on people being denied access to water or access to fertile land or a way to make a living or being denied their civil rights.
- Identify conflicts in the early stages and find ways to resolve them peacefully.
- Promote dialogue between people who have issues with each other. Dialogue frequently can set the stage for resolving conflicts.
- Involve a third party to help resolve differences when needed. Frequently a third party can make the difference between success or failure when people try to resolve a conflict.

- Forgive one another for mistakes that have been made. Without forgiveness, there is a large chance people will seek revenge.

Chapter 1 describes the personal and economic cost of violence. Chapter 2 outlines the various causes of violence. Chapters 3 through 6 explain the strategies for preventing violence. This includes preventing or modifying some of the underlying conditions, avoiding some of the triggering events, learning the skills needed to resolve conflicts, and resolving conflicts before they get out of hand. Chapters 7 through 10 describe some of the changes needed in our society and show how these same prevention strategies relate to preventing terrorism, international wars, and civil wars. Chapter 11 addresses some of the defensive strategies that have been tried and points out which ones seem to be helpful.

Some strategies can be implemented easily, and others will require a lot more time. Nevertheless, it is important to have a vision for the future and start the process of working toward the kind of world in which we want to live. If we do not start, we will never get there. Dr. Martin Luther King Jr. frequently said, "We shall either learn to live together as brothers and sisters, or we will perish together as fools. The choice is ours."

CHAPTER 1

—

The Cost of Violence

Violence results in a huge cost, and in most cases, it can be prevented. Violence breeds violence, and it frequently causes damage that cannot be repaired.

If a person is killed or injured physically or emotionally, there are many different costs involved. Some are easier to quantify than others. There are direct costs, indirect costs, and the cost of lost opportunities. There may be medical costs to treat the injuries or to determine the cause of death. There may be legal costs to gather evidence, prosecute the person responsible, and carry out the sentence imposed. Family members may have funeral expenses as well as emotional and financial hardships, resulting from the loss of a loved one, and if that loved one was providing financially for the family, he or she is no longer able to do so. The person responsible may have to stay in prison for years and not be able to provide income for the family. And of course, the loss of life or the suffering and limitations caused by serious injury may be hard to express in monetary terms. There also are emotional consequences of violence, and this can result in a lifetime of emotional and economic costs.

A human life is precious and cannot be replaced. Some violence can result in costs much broader than the ones listed above. When a child is killed in school, the other children as well as the faculty experience emotional trauma and disruption of their lives. When one person is killed or injured, that person's relatives or friends may seek revenge through violence. When a nation does something that results in violence to another nation, the nation being hurt might respond with violence. As you can see, violence frequently causes more violence.

The Centers for Disease Control and Prevention considers violence to be a public health problem, and they have an excellent website that shows the human and monetary costs of each type of violence with the following statistics:[1]

- In the United States, in 2020, there were 25,000 homicides, over 45,979 people died of suicide, and 1.1 million people were treated in emergency departments for assault.
- In the United States in 2020, there were 1,750 children who died of child abuse, and in 2018, the lifetime burden in the United States for child abuse was estimated to be $592 billion. (Lifetime burden means the cost incurred during the life of a person as a result of the damage done.)
- Elder abuse in the United States resulted in more than 643,000 older adults being treated in emergency departments from 2002 to 2016.
- Firearms violence in the United States in 2020 resulted in 45,222 deaths. More than half were suicides, and more than 4 in 10 were homicides.
- One in 5 women and one in 7 men in the United States have experienced severe physical violence from an intimate partner, and 1 in 5 homicide victims were killed by intimate partners. The lifetime economic cost of this is estimated to be $103,767 for each woman and $23,414 for each man.

Notes

[1] "Violence Prevention Home Page-CDC," Center for Disease Prevention, Revised September 2021, cdc.gov/violenceprevention/index.html./.

- More people suffer nonfatal firearm-related injuries than die. More than 7 out of every 10 medically treated firearm injuries are from firearm-related assaults. Nearly 2 out of every 10 are from unintentional firearm injuries.
- Homicide is the third leading cause of death for young people between the ages of 10 and 24, and it is the leading cause of death for non-Hispanic Black or African American youth. Each day, more than 1,000 youth are treated in emergency departments for physical assault–related injuries. Youth homicides and nonfatal physical assaults result in nearly $100 billion annually in medical and productivity costs alone, not including costs to the criminal justice system and psychological and social consequences.

Terrorism and wars also can be expensive. The attacks on the World Trade Center and the Pentagon on September 11, 2001, resulted in the deaths of 2,996 people and thousands of injuries, and people are still suffering and dying from exposure to the chemicals released by those attacks.

Then the United States declared war on terrorism and invaded Afghanistan and Iraq. These post-9/11 hostilities have continued to cause deaths. As of August 2021, it is estimated that "over 929,000 people have died in the post 9/11 wars due to direct war violence, and several times as many due to the reverberating effects of war." This includes over 387,000 civilians that have been killed as a result of the fighting. It also is estimated that these wars have resulted in 38 million war refugees and displaced persons. The United States federal price tag is over $8 trillion. "The wars have been accompanied by violations of human rights and civil liberties in the US and abroad such as torture and imprisonment without due process at Guantanamo."[2]

Casualties from these original attacks and the wars afterward could have been prevented if nonviolent practices had been used to deal with the issues in the early stages of hostilities.

---

[2] Watson Institute of International and Public affairs of Brown University, "Costs of War," September 2021, watson.brown.edu/costs/economic.

CHAPTER 2

—

The Causes of Violence

Any time someone commits an act of violence, that person could have chosen a nonviolent act instead. The factors leading up to a violent act can include things that just recently occurred as well as things that happened to that person throughout his entire life. As we look for ways to prevent violence, we must realize there are multiple factors to consider and multiple things that could have been done to prevent violence. Each preventive strategy we implement can be a valuable part of the overall solution.

Usually, a person commits an act of violence in response to some triggering event. Young children may strike out at one another because of jealousy or rivalry or revenge or because of bullying, and some people fail to grow out of this type of behavior. Other triggering events can include insults, threats, fear, anger, or pain. Also, the fear of losing power, wealth, affection, freedom, possessions, or pride can be a triggering event. Sometimes the triggering event is just the last straw in a whole sequence of events leading up to a crisis. Even seeing a weapon or gaining access to a weapon can be a triggering event. On the other hand, most people can encounter such triggering events without resorting to violence. The difference usually is caused by an underlying condition that makes it more likely for some people to choose a violent response.

Perhaps the most common underlying condition is the belief that violence is an appropriate way to respond to such triggering events. A lot of our values are developed during childhood. People who were abused as children are much more likely to be violent than children who were not abused.[1] James Gilligan, a psychiatrist who spent twenty-five years working with violent prison inmates, said all of these violent people he worked with had been seriously abused by their parents. He also said they committed acts of violence because they were shamed or disrespected by someone.[2] A lot of boys are taught they should respond to insults or threats with violence, or they will be considered cowards or sissies.

Several different things can cause a person to be predisposed to violence. There are biological causes such as genetics, medical or psychiatric diseases, or improper use of alcohol or other drugs. Some people have an information-processing deficit such as the tendency to view the actions of other people as hostile. There are psychological causes such as bipolar affective disorder, schizophrenia, major depression, general anxiety disorder, and antisocial personality disorder. There also are socioeconomic causes such as values and beliefs that are promoted in a family or the community or in peer groups or through the media, as well as through life experiences. It is important to recognize that these predisposing factors do not necessarily result in violence. They simply make it harder for a person to restrain violent impulses when faced with a triggering event.

With mass shootings, the perpetrator is usually driven by anger toward people who disrespected him, and he may be influenced by news reports of other mass shooters, and then he obtains access to the weapon or weapons for carrying out the act. Early warning signs may

Notes

[1] "Violence Prevention Home Page-CDC," Center for Disease Prevention, Revised September 2021, cdc.gov/violenceprevention/index.html.
[2] James Gilligan, *Preventing Violence* (New York, NY: Thames and Hudson Inc., 2001), 29–37.

include disruptive behavior, distressed behavior, behavior that causes others to be uncomfortable, and behavior that threatens others.[3]

Conflicts also can result in violence. Conflicts are a natural part of life, and they cannot be eliminated. However, conflicts do not have to result in violence. It is important for conflicts to be recognized in the early stages and dealt with appropriately. Here again, underlying conditions can influence whether or not a conflict can end peacefully.

With terrorism or civil unrest or international disputes, violence can result from oppression, deprivation, fear, political conflicts, national rivalry, a lust for power, religious fanaticism, disinformation, or greed. Also, remarks or actions can be perceived as hurtful and become triggering events because of cultural or racial differences that are misunderstood. National leaders and leaders of movements are human beings, and their decisions can be influenced by their own underlying conditions.

Another cause of violence is the way one act of violence causes subsequent acts of violence.

> Violence is highly contagious. Not only is it spread from the perpetrator of violence to the victim, but it is spread to onlookers and observers. It is not surprising that violent victimization leads to violent retaliation within and between families, peer groups, schools, communities, ethnic groups, cultures, and countries. What may be surprising to some is that simply the observation of violence also leads to increased violence within and between all of these groups. Violence can even be spread to far away people who observe it at a distance. The boundary of time and space

---

[3]   Jillian Peterson and James Densley, *The Violence Project: How to Stop a Mass Shooting Epidemic* (New York, NY: Abrams Press, 2021), 17–18 and 87.

that apply to most biological contagions do not
apply to the contagion of violence.[4]

The American Psychological Association issued a report listing
the primary causes of violence. Some of the main things listed were
a history of violence; inadequate child-rearing practices; attitudes
toward violence in society, poverty, socioeconomic inequality, prejudice, and discrimination; access to firearms, alcohol, drugs, and antisocial groups; violence in the mass media; and a dominant cultural
value that winning is everything.[5]

---

[4] L. Rowell Huesmann, "The Contagion of Violence: The Extent, the Process,
and the Outcome," Institute for Social Research, University of Michigan,
viewed December 30, 2022, ncbi.nlm.nih.gov/books/NBK189992/.

[5] Report of the American Psychological Association Commission on Violence
and Youth, Vol. I, "Violence and Youth," issued 1993, apa.org/pi/prevent-
violence/resources/violence-youth.pdf.

CHAPTER 3

———

Developing Values and Beliefs

One of the primary underlying conditions that predispose a person to violence is the belief that violence is an appropriate way to respond to insults or threats or other triggering events. If a child's family portrays violence as a normal or appropriate response to adversity, that child is likely to have a predisposition toward violence. If, instead, the child has parents who show the child love and acceptance and stability and bonding, teach by example and by words the importance of respecting and caring for other people, and teach by example and by words the importance of nonviolence, that child is likely to be less inclined toward violence.

As we consider prevention strategies, we might start with programs that teach school children how to be good parents and also teach new parents how to be good parents. Educational programs like this also could include several other values in addition to the importance of nonviolence. Here is a list of other values that could be taught to reduce violence and improve interpersonal relations in general:

> All people are to be treated with respect regardless of race, ethnicity, religion, political affiliation, education, economic condition, sexual preference, or disability. It is all right for peo-

ple to have different beliefs, different customs, and different ways of doing things as long as they respect the rights and well-being of other people. This is important because a lot of people have been taught that people of a different race or religion or some other characteristics are either dangerous or undesirable, and this prejudice frequently leads to violence.

Everyone makes mistakes, and we need to forgive people when they do and apologize when we do.

Actions and words have consequences, and it is a good idea to think about the possible consequences of the things we do or say.

Both women and men are to be treated with respect, not physically or emotionally abused. Being married does not give anyone the right to hurt or try to control their spouse.

No one has the right to force or coerce another person into sexual activity.

Human life is irreplaceable, and the taking of human life is devastating for that person's family and friends. Consequently, we must avoid actions that could kill or harm another person.

Firearms and other lethal implements must be handled with caution and stored safely. They should not be used to threaten or inflict wounds on people.

All of these values could be taught by parents as they nurture their children, and these values can be taught in schools, religious institutions, community centers, and a variety of nongovernmental organizations.

There are several good books about good parenting. One that begins with the care of newborns is *Nurse Peggy's Notes on Newborns:*

Caring for your New Baby by Margaret Sutton Wade.[1] Another is *Parent Effectiveness Training: The Proven Program for Raising Responsible Children*, by Thomas Gordon, which focuses on parent-child relationships a little later in the child's development.[2]

Children learn by example and by repetition. As a child observes the behavior of the parent, the child begins to adopt that behavior. Through repetition, the child develops automatic responses to the things happening in his environment. These automatic responses are developed through repetition, which builds up a sheath of material around the neurons connecting the stimulus to the response. If the parent uses violence against the child, the child will learn to use violence against others. One of the best ways to teach a parent how to discipline a child is to spend some time in the home, showing the parent how to discipline without violence because the parent also learns better by observing another person's behavior.[3]

A lot of parents still try to discipline children by spanking them even though this practice has been linked to obesity, lower IQ, and other health problems for the child, and studies have shown it causes the child to be more aggressive and have less impulse control.[4]

If a child has encountered adverse childhood experiences such as child abuse, family violence, food insecurity, discrimination, poverty, or trauma, other experiences in the child's life may help to reduce the chance of his becoming violent. The following list of questions is called "The Benevolent Childhood Experiences scale," and it will

---

Notes

[1] Margaret Sutton Wade, *Nurse Peggy's Notes on Newborns: Caring for Your New Baby* (Raleigh, NC: A Place to Copy, 2022).
[2] Thomas Gordon, Parent Effectiveness Training: The Tested New Way to Raise Responsible Children (New York, NY: Harmony Publishing, 2019).
[3] Rhea DuMont, Tom H. Hastings, and Emiko Noma, eds., *Conflict Transformation: Essays on Methods of Nonviolence* (Jefferson, NC: McFarland & Company Inc. Publishers, 2013), 202–204.
[4] DuMont, Hastings, and Noma, eds., *Conflict Transformation: Essays on Methods of nonviolence*, 205.

give you an idea of the other experiences that might help a child develop more normally:[5]

> Did you have at least one caregiver with whom you felt safe?
> Did you have at least one good friend?
> Did you have beliefs that gave you comfort?
> Did you like school?
> Did you have at least one teacher who cared about you?
> Did you have good neighbors?
> Was there an adult (not a parent/caregiver or the person from the first question) who could provide you with support and advice?
> Did you have opportunities to have a good time?
> Did you like yourself or feel comfortable with yourself?
> Did you have a predictable home routine, such as regular meals and a regular bedtime?

Each item on this list illustrates things all of us can do to help prevent a person from becoming violent.

Another value or belief that needs to change is the belief that violence is the appropriate response to violence. Whether we are considering children on the playground or gangs on the street or nations relating to nations, there is a widely held belief that the perpetrator needs to be taught a lesson, and a violent response is the best way to teach that lesson. Frequently, the violent response simply inflames more anger, and the hostility becomes worse.

Violence should not be ignored, and it should not be considered acceptable. However, there are many more effective ways to respond

---

[5] J. S. Merrick et al., "Benevolent Childhood Experiences (BCE) in Homeless Parents: A Validation and Replication Study," *Journal of Family Psychology*, 33, No.4 (2019): pp. 493–498.

to it. Choosing the appropriate response may require learning more about the cause of the violence. It could have been an accident. It could have been a misunderstanding. It could have been a bad decision that will never happen again. A good way to learn more about the cause is to initiate dialogue with the perpetrator. A lot of people are not willing to do this, but dialogue can be a helpful way to begin the process of mending a relationship. At some point, a third party may need to be involved. The problem may be resolved quickly, or it may require legal action. In either case, a nonviolent response has a much better chance of producing a good outcome.

Another widespread belief that can be problematic is the belief that talking with an adversary is a sign of weakness, and it is necessary to show strength through threats and demonstrations of power and violent actions to prevent aggression. I agree that some people and some nations will try to take advantage of others who seem to be unable or unwilling to defend themselves. It is important to have plans and means of self-defense. However, I am convinced that most people and most nations desire peace as long as they have access to the things they really consider important. If we want to live in peace with one another, we need to get to know one another and share ideas, aspirations, and concerns and jointly arrive at solutions that benefit all of us. This cannot happen if we constantly prevent communication and intensify hostile attitudes.

CHAPTER 4

Developing Skills for Implementation

Putting these values into practice requires a variety of skills. For example, people do not automatically know how to be good parents. It helps to grow up with good parents, but usually, additional instruction is needed.

Also, children need to learn how to resolve conflicts without violence. Each situation is different, so people need to think of several things that can be done to resolve conflicts peacefully. This usually involves listening to the other person and trying to understand their needs and their point of view. It helps to let the other person know you understand their point of view and that you respect them even if you do not agree with them. This can take creativity and practice. It is hard to respect someone who is being mean, disrespectful, or dangerous. It helps to recognize that such behavior is caused by something in that person's past, and if we can talk with them and listen to them, we may be able to understand the cause of this behavior and develop a way to change their attitude.

A study done in 1999 showed that children age four through eight could make significant improvements in their behavior by participating in games and role-play and discussions relating to real-life situations to improve their ability to think of alternative solutions to problems and to consider possible consequences of their actions. The study also showed significant improvements in child-rearing practices when these skills were taught to mothers of young children.[1]

If a person is yelling at you and threatening you, it will probably help to respond with a gentle voice and let them know you recognize they are upset. If they appear to be upset at you, you may need to apologize for the thing that caused their anger. Let them know you are willing to listen to their concern. You may not be able to solve the problem, but you can let them know you care, and you are willing to discuss the situation with them. There may be times when you need to walk away.

The Violence Project by Peterson and Densley describes a four-step model for de-escalating a situation in which a person may be about to become violent. This model can be summarized as follows:[2]

1. "De-escalate yourself. We cannot help someone else in crisis when we are escalated ourselves…The best way to De-escalate oneself is to take a few deep breaths, and brush off any negativity directed at us."
2. De-escalate the space around you. Someone in crisis should be in a private space, without others watching." It also helps to lower the lights, reduce noise and distractions, and be truly present with the person.
3. Use nonverbal communication. Use a soft voice and place yourself at eye level or lower than the person. It helps to sit down or kneel next to the person.
4. Actively listen. "The first step is what we say, but rather than saying anything in particular, it's most important to listen. Active listening involves deeply and authentically

---

Notes

1   Myrna B. Shure, "Preventing Violence the Problem-Solving Way," Office of Juvenile Justice and Delinquency Prevention, published April, 1999, https://ojjdp.ojp.gov/library/publications/preventing-violence-problem-solving-way.
2   Jillian Peterson, and James Densley, *The Violence Project: How to Stop a Mass Shooting Epidemic* (New York, NY: Abrams Press, 2021), pp. 66–67.

listening to another person with respect and without judgment or advice…The important part is focusing on their feelings…When we understand what someone is feeling, they feel seen and heard."

In our daily lives, there are a lot of things that can make us angry, and anger can easily lead to violence. Therefore, it is important to learn appropriate things we can do when we feel angry.

The most constructive way to deal with anger is to express it assertively without being aggressive, demanding, or disrespectful. This can be done by letting the other person know what your needs are and how your needs can be met without hurting anyone. You probably will have better results if you can do this in a way that focuses on how you feel and what caused these feelings instead of blaming the other person.

One technique for doing this is to use I-messages. These are statements structured in a way that focuses on what you are feeling and what you would like the other person to do differently. In other words, you start by saying "I feel…" (here, you state the way you feel). Then you say, "When you…" (here, you state what the other person has been doing that bothers you). Then you say, "Because…" (here, you state the impact that behavior has on you). Then you say, "And I would like…" (here, you explain what you want the other person to do differently). This type of statement focuses on what you are feeling and what you want to change without criticizing the other person and escalating the hostility.[3]

Another constructive response is to calm down. It may be helpful to pause and take three deep breaths before responding to the event that caused you to become angry. It is helpful to think about the consequences of anything you might say or do. It is better to wait until you have a chance to calm down and develop a constructive approach instead of responding in a way that escalates tensions.

---

[3] Carl Mirra, *United States Foreign Policy and the Prospect for Peace Education* (Jefferson, NC: McFarland & Company Inc., 2008), 154.

If a person is going to have access to firearms or other lethal items, they need instruction concerning the safe ways to handle and store these items. They also must be old enough and mentally and emotionally stable enough to handle this responsibility appropriately.

If you can spend time with people who are different racially or culturally or different in other ways, especially if you are engaging with them to work on a common goal or to participate together in recreation, that can give you a chance to understand them and see them as people who deserve respect and understanding. Also, sharing a meal with people of another race or religion can start the process of developing lasting friendships.[4]

Each of these values and skills can go a long way toward preventing violence. Efforts to teach these values and skills can be provided to children, young people, parents, religious institutions, community organizations, the media, legislators, and national leaders. A lot of resources are available for this purpose through the Centers for Disease Control and Prevention. If you search the Internet for CDC violence prevention, you will find the home page for the Violence Prevention Division of the Centers for Disease Control. There, you can select the type of violence you are interested in and learn how big the problem is, the consequences of the problem, risk and protective factors, prevention strategies, programs that have been implemented, and data concerning these programs' effectiveness.[5] Several states and private organizations also have valuable resources for this purpose. Some of these resources are listed in the bibliography.

Some of the approaches they recommend are as follows:

- Teach young people and young parents the importance of good parenting, and help them learn the skills required.

---

[4]   Robert S. Heaney, Zeyneb Sayilgan, and Claire Haymes, *Faithful Neighbors: Christian-Muslim Vision and Practice* (Harrisburg, PA: Morehouse Publishing, 2016).

[5]   Center for Disease Control, Violence Prevention Home Page, revised September 28, 2021, cdc.gov/violence prevention/index.html.

- Visit young mothers to make sure they have the information and resources they need to be good parents, and watch for signs of postpartum depression.
- Provide high-quality day care for children if both of their parents will be working out of the home.
- Provide preschool enrichment programs that involve the parents as well as the children.
- Teach skills in social/emotional learning, safe dating practices, and family relationships.
- Connect youth with caring adults, and provide activities such as mentoring and after-school programs.
- Provide services to lessen the negative effect of adverse childhood experiences and substance abuse problems.
- Include community-based organizations in the planning and operation of programs to educate children and parents concerning alternatives to violence.
- Reduce the stigma around seeking help with parenting or substance abuse, depression, or suicidal thoughts.
- Encourage the use of a third party to help resolve conflicts. The book by William Ury entitled *The Third Side: Why We Fight and How We Can Stop* is an excellent resource for showing how important it is to involve a third party in resolving conflict. For example, a third party can provide resources, teach strategies, mediate, repair injured relationships, and establish guidelines for dialogue.[6]
- Promote safe, stable, nurturing relationships and environments where children live, learn, and play.
- Teach skills in conflict resolution or skills in conflict transformation, which focuses on changing the underlying cause of the problem. This may include skills in organizing support, publicizing grievances, and developing nonviolent strategies for promoting change.

---

[6] William Ury, *The Third Side: Why We Fight and How We Can Stop* (New York, NY: Penguin Books, 2000).

- Teach skills in dialogue. For dialogue to be productive, each participant must be willing to listen with an open mind. The purpose of dialogue is not to debate or negotiate. The purpose is to begin to understand the other person's point of view and the reasons for that point of view. Once the two parties understand each other, it will be much easier to find common ground and possibly a path toward resolving the problem. Usually, if people have a very strong disagreement concerning an issue, there is an element of truth on each side. There is something of value on each side worth considering. By seriously looking at the positive and negative aspects of each side, it may be possible to arrive at a solution that is better than either original position.

- Even with suicide, many of the same prevention strategies still apply. For example, it is still important to recognize emotional problems in their early stages and to take steps to resolve them before they become a crisis. Dialogue also is important, but with suicide, the perpetrator and the victim are the same person, so dialogue frequently needs to be with another person who has the skills to be helpful. Some suicides result from bullying either in person or on social media. This situation can be prevented by teaching people to treat all people with respect.

- We also have a lot of veterans who commit suicide as a result of PTSD or traumatic brain injury or have difficulty adjusting to civilian life after being in combat. Prevention strategies include preventing wars and providing more help for veterans returning to civilian life. Suicide also can be caused by stress or financial problems or financial inequality or other situations that cause the person to feel hopeless or shamed. Some people react to this by striking out at others, while some strike out at themselves. Consequently, preventing these situations or helping a person overcome them prevents both of these violent responses.

The National Institute of Mental Health provides a good set of risk factors for suicide as well as warning signs, action steps, and types of treatment and therapies.[7] There is a long list of warning signs, including talking about wanting to die, feeling hopeless, and being a burden to others. The action steps to take are to ask if the person is thinking about killing themselves, reducing access to lethal items or places, listening carefully, acknowledging their feelings, helping them call 988 for the Suicide and Crisis Lifeline, and staying in touch after a crisis.

---

[7] "Suicide Prevention," National Institute of Mental Health, revised September 26, 2022, www.nimh.nih.gov/suicideprevention.

CHAPTER 5

—

Other Underlying Conditions

When individuals or national leaders resort to violence, that decision was influenced not only by the triggering event but also by all of the various underlying conditions acquired during the life of the person or people making that decision. As mentioned in chapters 3 and 4, the primary factors are the values and beliefs of the people involved and the skills they have for solving conflicts peacefully. On the other hand, several other underlying conditions may impact that decision.

Economic Factors

If a person is struggling to meet the economic needs of the family, this can create a lot of stress and make them less able to deal with triggering events. Economic difficulties also can cause parents to work more hours and have less time to care for their children. It also can limit their ability to afford things the children need.

Growing up in poverty, while observing other families with excessive wealth, can increase a person's feeling of shame and the likelihood of violence.

> On a worldwide basis, the nations with the
> highest inequalities in wealth and income…have

the highest homicide rates (and also the most collective or political violence). Among the developed nations, the United States has the highest inequalities in wealth and income, and also has by far the highest homicide rates, five to ten times higher than the other first world nations, all of which have the lowest levels of inequality and relative poverty in the world, and the lowest homicide rates.[1]

Prevention strategies might include job training, budgeting, financial assistance, and policies that help increase income for low-income families. We also might look at policies used by other countries to decrease income inequality.

Social and Cultural Factors

If a young person does not have opportunities for adventure and self-fulfillment and a sense of belonging, he is more likely to join a gang or, in other ways, be influenced by peer groups, and this can increase his chances of using alcohol or drugs or participating in violence. Preventive strategies might include mentoring, after-school activities, sports, part-time-jobs, or the arts.

If a person is in prison, a mental institution, or a nursing home, his freedom is limited, his choices for self-fulfillment are limited, his privacy is restricted, and he is part of a larger group that also is experiencing these same problems. All of these factors increase the likelihood of aggressive behavior. Preventive strategies might include activities like sports, the arts, entertainment, or hobbies.

Notes

[1] James Gilligan, *Preventing Violence* (New York, NY: Thames and Hudson Inc., 2001), 39.

Some veterans have trouble adjusting to life after combat, and this sometimes results in violence. Also, some football players have an increased incidence of spouse abuse. There are a variety of possible causes for these problems such as PTSD or traumatic brain injury or possibly training in aggressive behavior. Preventive strategies might include reducing the number of wars in which people are exposed to trauma, modifying sports to prevent head injuries, and providing counseling and therapy relating to this problem before it develops and afterward.

Intimate partners may develop jealousy or fear of abandonment or control issues that can lead to violence. Preventive strategies might include counseling on how to improve the relationship or assistance in getting out of the relationship.

A young mother may be so stressed with childcare in addition to other responsibilities that she strikes out at the child. The father also may hurt the child because it is disrupting his daily life in ways he does not know how to handle. Prevention strategies might include counseling in parenting skills and providing periodic relief from childcare such as respite care, day care, or temporary foster care.

In some situations, frustration can accumulate over time in what is called an incubation period. For example, a child who is feeling lonely and ignored by his peers may eventually start causing trouble in class or looking for illegal ways to become noticed. Prevention strategies might include watching for this type of situation so it can be dealt with before it becomes too bad.

Some people develop resentment or hatred for categories of people because of experiences they encountered with one or more people in that category or because they were taught people like that were evil or undesirable in some way. This might be based on race, ethnicity, religion, or other factors. Prevention strategies might include exposing people to other races and cultures and religions by letting them work together toward common goals through sports, employment, school, or other activities.

Some employment situations are very stressful, and over time, hostility toward the employer or other workers can build up. Preventive strategies might include arranging for the employer to understand the importance of this situation so he can make changes in the work environment or the work requirements to reduce stress. For parents who are employed, it can be very helpful for them to have some flexibility concerning work hours and time off.

Biological Factors

As we consider biological factors, we realize there are still unanswered questions concerning which personal characteristics are determined by genetics and which are influenced more by the environment, so we do not need to make a distinction there. On the other hand, we do know it is important for a woman to be healthy and have good prenatal care to have the best possible outcome for her baby, and that can help prevent some of the possible underlying conditions.

We do know males are much more likely to be violent than females because of the increased testosterone and also perhaps because of societal expectations.

Some people who have intellectual deficiency may have more tendency to become violent when they are in challenging situations because they have more trouble dealing with the situation. On the other hand, these people are more likely to be the victims of violence than the perpetrators.

People who have an imbalance of serotonin or dopamine also may have more tendency to become violent in stressful situations.

If the frontal cortex of the brain is not functioning well, or if there are lesions or changes in the brain that can limit the ability to control aggression, this can be a problem.

Traumatic brain injury can be caused by military injuries or sporting events or intimate partner abuse or other incidents. This can predispose a person to violence.

People who are experiencing severe pain or difficulty breathing or extreme cold also may become more aggressive.

Several drugs also can increase aggressive behavior. Examples are alcohol, mescaline, peyote, ecstasy, LSD, angel dust, steroids, and some drugs used to treat Parkinson's disease.

Prevention strategies can be directed toward preventing the development of the condition in the first place. An example would be preventing traumatic brain injury or preventing the use of steroids to enhance performance in sports. Also, providing good prenatal care and nutrition can help to prevent some biological deficits.

Another preventive strategy would be treatment of the condition to eliminate it or reduce the effect. An example could be providing medication or surgery or training in management.

Another approach might be to help the person learn how to avoid triggering events or how to deal with them more appropriately and how to reduce stress.

Psychological Factors

Some of the psychological diagnoses that increase the chance of violence include bipolar affective disorder, schizophrenia, various types of dementia, posttraumatic stress disorder, personality disorders, intermittent explosive disorder, attention-deficit/hypertension disorder, antisocial personality, postpartum depression, and borderline personality. Most people who have mental health problems do not become violent. Sometimes their behavior causes other people to become violent toward them.

On the other hand, psychological problems can be an underlying condition that becomes one of the factors leading to a violent response. A normal healthy person has empathy for other people and would resist the temptation to kill someone because of this empathy and the knowledge of the guilt that would result. "A study conducted by the US Army during the Second World War…found that only fifteen to twenty percent of soldiers would fire on enemies." Its chief investigator, Brigadier General S. L. A. Marshall, concluded that "the average healthy individual will not of his own volition take a life."

Therefore, the army indoctrinated the soldiers to deny the humanity of the enemy and to increase contempt for the enemy.[2]

Prevention strategies for psychological problems might include identifying and treating the condition. Also, children whose behavior indicates they might need help learning how to relate more appropriately with other children could be identified and offered assistance. In other words, we do not need to wait until a child has a psychological diagnosis before providing help. Some children have a conduct disorder, are disruptive in class, or cause problems for other children. There also are children who are loners and fail to develop social interaction skills. Some children frequently are subjected to bullying. In each of these situations, it can be helpful for someone to talk with the child and find out if the child needs help learning how to interact more appropriately. This may prevent the development of a psychological disorder or provide an opportunity for early intervention. Other preventive strategies might include treating the condition, finding ways to limit triggering events, teaching kids not to be bullies, and teaching skills in how to handle conflict and stress.

Each person is different. Some people are noticeably different from the norm for biological, social, or psychological reasons. Some of these people learn how to accept their difference and even thrive by using their difference to their advantage. Others are ashamed of their difference, and it becomes a problem for them. It is helpful if we can teach people to accept things about themselves that cannot be changed and to make the most of the qualities they possess. It also is helpful if we can accept and respect people even if they have noticeable differences.

---

[2] Carl Mirra, *United States Foreign Policy and the Prospect for Peace Education* (Jefferson, NC: McFarland & Company Inc., 2008), 85.

CHAPTER 6

Recognizing Problems Early

A large amount of violence in this world results from conflicts that are not resolved peacefully. This includes international disputes, civil unrest, terrorism, domestic violence, workplace violence, and gang violence. The longer these conflicts continue, the harder they will be to resolve because each side becomes more and more frustrated, and each side becomes more and more hostile toward the other side. Especially if violence occurs, it becomes even harder to solve the problem because the violence has added another issue that complicates the process of negotiation.

Identifying a problem in the early stages can be done in a variety of ways, depending on the situation. If you are involved in the conflict, you can take the initiative to promote a dialogue with the other party or find a third party that can help arrange a dialogue. If the conflict does not involve you but involves someone else whom you know, you might talk with that person about the importance of resolving the problem before it gets worse. If you are skilled in conflict resolution, you might offer to help resolve a conflict, whether it is between individuals or some kind of group. If you become aware of a person or group experiencing oppression, deprivation, or some other kind of grievance, you might talk with them about the importance of resolving the problem peacefully and help them explore ways to do that. If you become aware of an international conflict that involves your country, you might urge your government to work toward a diplomatic solution. As you can see, there are a lot of ways you can help to prevent violence.

One way to identify these problems in the early stages is to make sure a lot of people are watching and listening for indications of conflict. People in leadership positions have a responsibility for this, but they may have a biased view and not consider the problem important. People who feel oppressed, deprived, or not listened to have a responsibility to speak out, but their complaints may not get results. The media may be able to help with the problem, and there may also be public or private organizations that watch for such problems and bring them to the attention of people who can help.

Each of us can take part in preventing violence by watching and listening for conflicts that need to be resolved—for example, children who are being bullied at school, children who are being abused, women who are abused by their husbands or boyfriends, employers who mistreat their employees, neighborhoods that do not get adequate service from their government, nations that have border disputes, nations that oppress minority populations, etc.

As conflicts are identified, there are a lot of ways to try to resolve them. The simplest approach is to encourage dialogue between the parties involved. It may be helpful to involve a third party to help facilitate discussion and explore possible solutions. In some cases, legal action may be needed. Each situation is different, so strategies must be based on the situation.

CHAPTER 7

Changes Needed in Our Society

Several things could be done to decrease the amount of violence in our society. This includes changes in family structure, schools, the media, legislation, law enforcement, prisons, income disparities, and public attitudes. There are also global issues that need to be addressed.

A lot of the needed changes to prevent violence require legislative action, but political leaders in this country have become so polarized that it is hard for them to open their minds to productive discussions with one another. There is a tendency for each to demonize the other, and progress on issues is very difficult. This is also made much worse by misinformation spread by some news media and by social media. Consequently, broad portions of the public believe things that are not true, and some are being incited to violence. We need to find ways to change this. One organization that is trying to improve this situation is Braver Angels. The organization describes itself as follows:

> We are a national movement to bridge the partisan divide. We are equally divided between conservatives and progressives at every level of leadership. We work in communities, on college campuses, in the media, and in the halls of political power. Our strength comes from our mem-

bers and most of our work is done by patriotic
volunteers.[1]

In the United States, the family structure has changed in a way
that gives parents less opportunity to provide adequate childcare.
According to US census data, the percentage of households with
married couples and children dropped from 45 percent in 1960 to
23 percent in the year 2000.

> In 1998, 12.8 million households were
> headed by single mothers. More than half of first
> births were to single women. Of children grow-
> ing up in single-mother homes, 60 percent are
> living in poverty as compared to 11 percent in
> two-parent homes.[2]

This makes it much harder for children to get the care they
need, and it increases their exposure to the risks of economic inequality. Of course, some single mothers can provide adequately for their
children, but many find this to be very difficult.

The American Psychological Association issued a report that
described several features of good intervention programs to prevent
violence. Some of these recommendations can be summarized as
follows:[3]

- Provide home visitors for at-risk families, including prenatal and postnatal counseling.

Notes

[1] "Braver Angels," accessed January 01, 2023, braverangels.org.
[2] Rhea DuMont, Tom H. Hastings, and Emiko Noma, eds., *Conflict Transformation: Essays on Methods of Nonviolence* (Jefferson, NC: McFarland & Company Inc. Publishers, 2013), 202.
[3] Report of the American Psychological Association Commission on Violence and Youth, Vol. I, "Violence and Youth," issued 1993, apa.org/pi/prevent-violence/resources/violence-youth.pdf.

- Provide preschool programs that address intellectual, emotional, and social needs and the development of cognitive and decision-making processes.
- Provide school-based programs for children and adolescents promoting social and cognitive skills.
- For high-risk or predelinquent youth, work with and modify the family system.
- Interventions to prevent and treat sexual violence are very important.
- Seriously violent youth need treatment involving the school, parents, teachers, peers, and community.

Schools and community organizations need to teach values as described in chapter 3 as well as conflict resolution skills, and they need to have resources for identifying and helping children who have problems with social and emotional development. They also need to provide more opportunities for young people to find self-fulfillment, adventure, and a sense of belonging without turning to gangs, drug use, and other destructive behavior.

It would help if TV programs, movies, and video games had less violence and more examples of nonviolent ways to respond to adversity. Research has shown that prolonged exposure to violence on TV results in more violence.[4] In the United States and several other nations, there is a tendency to glorify people who are warriors and people who violently save the day. Perhaps it would be possible to put more emphasis on people who use nonviolence to solve problems and show how that can be done.

Over the last several decades, the income gap and wealth gap between the poor and the wealthy have grown tremendously. More and more people are finding it hard to make ends meet financially. This produces stress, which frequently leads to violence. More opportunities need to be available for disadvantaged people to get medical insurance, job training, higher education, childcare, employment, and employee-friendly workplaces. As mentioned in chapter 5, we

---

4   DuMont, Conflict Transformation: Essays on Methods of Nonviolence, 205.

might want to look at policies used by other countries to reduce income inequality in the United States.

Law enforcement officers have a responsibility that can be overwhelming. They are given the responsibility of enforcing the laws and protecting the public. Frequently, they have to make split-second decisions about whether to use violence to protect themselves and others or to use some other response to the threats they are facing. They do not have the facts needed for such a decision until it is too late. We need to make sure people recruited to serve in law enforcement are not predisposed to violence and do not have hostile attitudes toward segments of the population. We also need to make sure they are trained to respect all people and to practice methods of approaching people in a way that is safe but not threatening, if possible. They also need to be trained in ways to reduce tension in stressful situations.

Prisons frequently have a detrimental effect on the people who are incarcerated. Instead of being correctional institutions, they frequently expose inmates to the influence of more hardened criminals and make it harder for inmates to be successful members of society when they are released. James Gilligan, in his book *Preventing Violence*, recommends two basic changes to the prison system. He recommends that offenders who are not violent should not be sent to prison but disciplined in some other way. Of course, offenders who really pose a threat to the public need to be restrained, but not punished. He proposes the use of what he calls antiprisons, which would be "a locked, secure residential college, whose purpose and function would be educational and therapeutic, not punitive." His reasoning is that punishment is perceived as violence, and it is important for these offenders to be treated with respect and not violence because they need to learn a different way of behaving through the way they are treated.[5]

In this country, we are blessed to have a constitution that ensures freedom of speech and freedom of assembly, and we have

---

[5] James Gilligan, *Preventing Violence* (New York: Thames and Hudson Inc., 2001), 114–130.

laws that protect the right of people to criticize the government or businesses. Sometimes such protests are accompanied by violence against property or people. It is essential that we protect the right of people to protest, but it has been shown that protests can be much more effective if they do not involve violence. Nonviolent protests have been very effective in correcting numerous social problems, and we need to encourage protesters to be well organized and trained in nonviolent procedures.

Firearm-related injuries are among the five leading causes of death for people ages one to sixty-four in the United States. Sixty percent of these are suicides, and 30 percent are homicides.[6] In 2013, Johns Hopkins University involved more than twenty experts from several disciplines to study ways of reducing gun violence in America. This group presented very specific recommendations that can be summarized as follows:

> Improve the background check system to make it more effective.
> Prevent high-risk people from buying guns.
> Improve the laws and enforcement of laws concerning the sale of firearms.
> Ban the future sale of assault weapons and large-capacity ammunition magazines.
> Provide funding for research to understand the causes and solutions of gun violence.[7]

Violence against women and girls is a problem in the United States and is even more of a problem in several other countries. Globally, one in three women experiences physical and/or sexual intimate partner violence or nonpartner sexual violence in her lifetime. As a result, many of them have suffered from depression, anxiety, unplanned pregnancies, sexually transmitted diseases, and HIV.

---

[6] Daniel W. Webster and Jon S. Vernick, eds., *Reducing Gun Violence in America* (Baltimore, MD: The Johns Hopkins University Press, 2013).

[7] Daniel W. Webster and Jon S. Vernick, eds., *Reducing Gun Violence in America*.

Many have also become unable to work or care for themselves or their children. They also have higher rates of miscarriage and low-birth-weight children, as well as higher rates of infant and child mortality. Their children have also suffered emotionally.[8] "Globally 47,000 women and girls were killed by their intimate partners or other family members in 2020."[9]

Efforts are being made to prevent these problems, but progress is slow. The strategies are to improve the safety of women, change unequal power relationships, start changing attitudes early in life, and enact and enforce new laws and policies.

At least two hundred million women and girls aged fifteen to forty-nine have undergone female genital mutilation (FGM), and in some countries, at least nine in ten women aged fifteen to forty-nine have been mutilated in this way.[10] This is a traumatic experience for the girls, and it can result in very serious long-term medical consequences. "Treatment of health complications of FGM in 27 high prevalence countries is estimated to cost 1.4 billion dollars USD per year and is projected to rise to 2.3 billion USD by 2047 if no action is taken."[11]

Violence against women and girls is a cultural problem, and a lot of it can be prevented by education and legislation. A lot of boys and young men have not been taught the importance of respecting women and girls, and they do not understand the devastating consequences their actions have for the girls and possibly for themselves. Education needs to start with the parents and then be reinforced in the schools and the community. In many other countries, legislation

---

[8] "Violence against Women," World Health Organization, updated March 9, 2021, WHO.int/news-room/fact-sheet/detail/violence-against-women.

[9] "Killing of Women and Girls by Their Intimate Partners or Other Family Members," United Nations Office of Drugs and Crime, updated November 2021, UNodc.org/documents/data-and-analysis/statistics/crime/UN_BriefFem_251121.pdf.

[10] Sarah Ferguson, "Take Action to Eliminate Female Genital Mutilation Now," UNICEF USA, created February, 5, 2019, unicefusa.org/stories/take-action-eliminate-female-genital-mutilation-now.

[11] "Female Genital Mutilation," World Health Organization, updated January 21, 2002, who.int/news-room/fact-sheets/detail/female-genital-mutilation.

is needed, and social norms will need to be changed. This may be a very slow process.

As mentioned in chapter 5, stress and economic inequality can be underlying causes of violence. On a global scale, two processes that tend to increase both stress and economic inequality are population growth and global warming.

Global warming is causing sea levels to rise and changing weather conditions in ways that increase human migration and food shortages. This will continue to get worse if the trend is not reversed, and this causes more stress and the potential for conflict in the world.

In 1950, the world birth rate was five births per woman, and in 2021, it had dropped to 2.3 births per woman. This is encouraging, but the birth rate is highest in undeveloped countries in Africa and several countries in Southeast Asia. Meanwhile, most of the wealth is in the United States and other developed countries, so that means the stress of population growth will mostly be on populations that are least able to deal with it.[12]

Global warming and population growth, as well as civil strife within nations, are causing a lot of people to migrate because they either cannot obtain the resources they need to sustain life or are threatened by violence in their own nations. These problems are getting worse, and there needs to be a willingness on the part of the international community to help people in these situations and to reverse the trends causing the problems. These are our neighbors, and we have a responsibility to provide help if we can. In addition to our moral obligation to help refugees, we are also bound to do so under international law as specified in the United Nations 1951 Refugee Convention.[13]

---

[12] Joseph J. Bish, "A Breakdown of the United Nations World Population Prospects 2022 Report," created July 14, 2022.

[13] "Resolution 2198 (XXI) adopted by the United Nations General Assembly," UNHCR, accessed January 1, 2023, unhcr.org/en-us/3b66c2aa10.

CHAPTER 8

—

Terrorism

Terrorism, whether domestic or international, usually happens when a person or group of people feels frustrated because they think they are being treated unjustly and are not able to resolve the problem through normal legal procedures. We can prevent this by recognizing the problem in its early stages and taking steps to resolve it before it becomes violent. This requires a willingness to listen to the complaints and indications of frustration in the neighborhood, nation, and other nations. We need to know what caused dissatisfaction. We need to develop opportunities for dialogue so the people with problems have a chance to explain their grievances and we have a chance to let them know we understand. Then we need to jointly look for ways to resolve the problem.

Just like with personal violence, the problem lies in one party disrespecting another party, the conflict not being resolved early, and the injured party failing to use nonviolent tactics to express their frustration. There is also a failure for the parties involved to develop a value system based on respect for each other and to value human life. This is even more difficult to resolve if the party in power is authoritarian and uses violent tactics to silence discontent.

History has shown that nonviolence can work to resolve serious conflicts. Examples include the tactics used by Mahatma Gandhi in India, the tactics used by Dr. Martin Luther King Jr. in the United

States, the process used by Nelson Mandela in South Africa, and the process that led to peace in Northern Ireland. Sometimes a nonviolent protest is met by violence, and if the protest responds with violence, serious civil war can result. This happened in Syria and Yemen.

Solutions may be difficult and may take a long time, but if our government is working together with the people who are frustrated, the chance of success is increased, and the chance of violence is decreased. If violence has already occurred, the situation becomes more complicated. There is a tendency to punish the violence and not solve the underlying problem because we do not want to reward the violence. That is one reason nonviolent tactics are much more productive than violent tactics. On the other hand, if the underlying problems are not dealt with, the people who are frustrated will continue to be frustrated, and the violence is likely to persist. As an example, some people in Palestine have continued to violently attack Israel for decades, and their grievances still have not been resolved. Likewise, the Israelis have continued to respond with violence, and that has not stopped the attacks on them. This pattern of behavior cannot solve the problems for either side.

The only hope for peace is for the Israeli government and the people who are attacking them to sit down together and discuss ways to resolve their differences. The belief that one cannot negotiate with an enemy is standing in the way of progress. Some political leaders think a discussion with the enemy is a sign of weakness and rewards the enemy's bad behavior. Instead, discussions with the enemy can be the beginning step in a long process of changing bad behavior and setting the stage for understanding each other's needs.

For the Israelis and Palestinians to find peace, there will need to be significant changes on both sides. For example, it will be hard for the Israelis to trust the Palestinians and feel safe from attack unless the Palestinians agree to refrain from any subsequent attacks. On the other hand, the Palestinians will need some assurance that they will have good access to water and all the things necessary for making a living and will be able to govern themselves and be free from occupation. These changes will not be possible unless there can be forgiveness and reconciliation on both sides because both sides have

36

suffered for a long time and there is a lot of anger and hatred to be overcome. There are also a lot of additional issues to be worked out.

The conflict between Israel and Palestine is a good example of a situation in which a third party needs to be involved. A lot of progress has been made in the fields of mediation and conflict transformation, especially in situations involving different cultures. The United States would not be a good third party because the United States is viewed as being biased toward Israel. To be effective, the mediator or mediators would need to be unbiased and must be careful to include all of the stakeholders in the process, including the people on both sides who may be viewed as terrorists or extremists.

In the United States, there are several issues that cause some people to become emotionally upset and sometimes resort to violence. Some examples are abortion, white supremacy, immigration, police brutality, and possession of firearms. These issues have been intensified by a lot of false information distributed by social media and some news outlets. This has resulted in many people distrusting the government and most conventional news outlets. If these beliefs and feelings are not dealt with, there are likely to be more people who resort to violence.

Our political leaders need to recognize the importance of honest dialogue and legislation to help people distinguish between fact and fiction. There needs to be a willingness to listen to both sides and to recognize that the truth is more important than political party. We already have experienced several instances of domestic terrorism because of this problem, and we do not need to let this problem get worse. Democracy requires dialogue and compromise. Both sides must be willing to engage in honest discussions.

This is also a situation in which a third party may be necessary to bridge the gap between the two sides. I would suggest that for each of these issues, a bipartisan committee be established in congress, and with the help of expert mediators, these committees meet to work on these issues. It will be important to include people with very differing views on these committees and to allow enough time for thorough discussions in which each side can fully express their views. Once an agreement is reached, it will be important to fully inform the public concerning the decisions made and the reasons for the decisions. It will take time for some segments of the public to accept the decisions, but this could be a very important first step in the process.

International terrorism has also been a problem. Of course, the government is responsible for bringing the terrorists to justice and preventing subsequent attacks. On the other hand, if this is done through violent means, frequently, there are innocent civilian casualties, and this can make the situation worse instead of better. We would not tolerate such actions in our homeland, so why should we carry out such actions in another country? Instead of invading Afghanistan and Iraq, the United States could have used the international legal system to apprehend and prosecute the terrorists. This was done when Ramzi Yousef bombed the World Trade Center in 1993. Using the international legal system after the 9/11 attacks would have resulted in much less cost, fewer lives lost, and much better relations with other nations, and it would not have created more terrorists.

Then, the United States could have put more effort into identifying the things that cause people to become terrorists and finding ways to reverse this process. Resolving conflict in the early stages is much more productive than waiting until angry people have committed terrorist acts. We need to sit down with people from other countries and find out what needs to be changed to deal with this anger. We may not be able to change their minds, but at least we should be able to understand the problems and learn how to make friends instead of enemies.

Osama bin Laden gave the following explanation of his reason for hating the United States of America:

1. US troops were on Saudi soil, thus desecrating holy ground;
2. the US invaded Iraq and waged the Persian Gulf War;
3. Palestinians had been evicted from their homeland and IDF occupying troops were in Palestine; and

4. US support for corrupt regimes in Muslim nations, begin-
    ning with Saudi Arabia.[1]

People in the United States may not think these issues justify
the terrorist acts committed, but this is an example of cultural differences, which can be devastating when ignored.

A similar example was the United States' support of the Shah
of Iran while he executed his opponents. This caused Iranians to
consider Americans terrorists and crusaders occupying the holy land
and led to the 1979 kidnapping of US citizens.[2] One of the reasons
Islamist terrorists hate the United States is expressed in this quotation from a 2004 report of a federal advisory committee established
to provide independent advice to the Secretary of Defense referring
to Islamist terrorists:

> If there is one overarching goal they share,
> it is the overthrow of what Islamists call the
> "apostate" regimes: the tyrannies of Egypt, Saudi
> Arabia, Pakistan, Jordan, and the Gulf states.
> They are the main targets of the broader Islamist
> movements, as well as the actual fighter groups.
> The United States finds itself in the strategically
> awkward and potentially dangerous situation of
> being the longstanding prop and alliance partner
> of these authoritarian regimes. Without the US
> these regimes could not stand.[3]

The United States has intervened in the internal affairs of other
countries over fifty times in the last half century, and it accounts

---

Notes

[1] Tom Hastings, *Nonviolent Response to Terrorism* (Jefferson, NC: McFarland &
     Company Inc. Publishers, 2004), 16–17.
[2] Hastings, Nonviolent Response to Terrorism, 17.
[3] Carl Mirra, *United States Foreign Policy and the Prospects for Peace Education*
     (Jefferson, NC: McFarland & Company Inc. Publishers, 2008), 108.

for 50 percent of global arms sales. Frequently, these arms are used by these nations to silence dissent in these countries and deny basic human rights to their citizens.[4]

"Working to change the environment in which terrorism is created is the best defense against future terrorism and that defense relies upon creative, compassionate, persistent nonviolence in every aspect of our individual and national behavior."[5] Frequently, terrorism is the result of people being deprived of their homeland or their ability to obtain the necessities of life. For example, Palestinians have been denied access to their homeland and water; Syrians have been denied access to water; and Kurds have been divided into minority populations in the various nations surrounding them, where they are denied basic human rights.

This does not excuse the violence carried out by terrorists; it simply indicates the need to recognize the conflicts and resolve them before violence happens or find ways to resolve the problems causing the violence.

The practice of denying rights to people who are of a different ethnic, religious, or racial identity and inflaming hatred against such people is one of the primary causes of violence. Some countries use their public education systems to promote such hatred and negative views. If this practice can be reversed so that public attitudes of acceptance and respect can be promoted, this will help reduce violence.

In his book *Nonviolent Response to Terrorism*, Tom Hastings says,

> There is no realistic response until the law has been invoked and enforced-whether that is a basic law of murder used against Timothy McVeigh or various international laws and domestic laws against members of al-Qaida. Then we have to turn to the negotiation strategy,

---

[4]   Mirra, United States Foreign Policy and the Prospects for Peace Education, 28.
[5]   Hastings, Nonviolent Response to Terrorism, 204.

which may well include significant alterations of US foreign policy.[6]

We need to practice both justice and forgiveness.

---

[6] Hastings, Nonviolent Response to Terrorism, 204.

CHAPTER 9

—

International Conflicts

International violence can be caused or prevented in much the same way as personal violence. Typically, there is a disagreement, and adequate steps are not taken to resolve the conflict in the early stages. Just like with personal violence, the problem frequently lies in the leaders of one nation feeling disrespected by the leaders of another nation or being afraid the other nation will take advantage of them. This becomes even more of a problem if one nation has a value system that prefers violent tactics to nonviolent ones. Unfortunately, the stakes are much higher in an international conflict. On the other hand, nations are controlled by people, and the same values and skills can be helpful to influence their decisions and actions.

Here again, it is important to recognize the problem in the early stages and arrange a dialogue in which each side listens to the concerns of the other side. This process may be more difficult because there may be differences in language, culture, values, and political philosophies. It may be necessary to utilize a third party to help bridge the gap between the two sides. It will be helpful if each side can try to understand the point of view of the other side. If the problem festers until violence starts, it will be much harder to resolve.

Frequently, there is a need for the two sides to spend time together and get to know each other personally before trying to negotiate a solution. It is also helpful for each side to talk about the specific issues they see as a problem instead of insisting on a specific solution. It may be helpful if both parties use I-messages as described in chapter 4 to express their grievances.

One example of success concerning international negotiations was the Camp David Accords in 1978, in which President Jimmy Carter worked with Egyptian President Anwar Sadat and Israeli Prime Minister Menachem Begin to develop a peace treaty between the two countries. This demonstrated the importance of involving a third party in the process.

Another example is the Strategic Arms Reduction Treaty between the United States and the Soviet Union, which resulted in the removal of about 80 percent of all strategic nuclear weapons then in existence. This long negotiating process started in 1969 as the Strategic Arms Limitation Talks and continued until 1991, when the Strategic Arms Reduction Treaty was signed. This demonstrated the importance of persistence and interpersonal relations.

International conflicts will be much easier to resolve if we can develop international laws that can be enforced by the community of nations. I would suggest the following:

1. No nation will violently attack or invade another nation.
2. Disputes concerning national boundaries will be settled through arbitration.
3. Each nation will be responsible for its own form of government, and other nations will not interfere with the internal political practices of another nation.
4. If any nation needs help securing essential resources, other nations will provide assistance based on internationally agreed-upon criteria.
5. If the residents of a nation are being mistreated by their own government, the problem can be referred to an international body that will investigate the situation and recommend a solution.
6. No nation should unilaterally try to control another nation.

It will probably be hard to get nations to agree to these require-ments, and the requirements may need to be modified as they are dis-cussed. On the other hand, war is horrible and expensive. Some kind of international agreement needs to be reached that will effectively enable each nation to be safe from invasion and each international dispute to be resolved peacefully.

The United Nations has already made a lot of progress in this direction. In 1945, the Charter of the United Nations included the following statement:

> All Members shall refrain in their interna-tional relations from the threat or use of force against the territorial integrity or political inde-pendence of any state, or in any other manner inconsistent with the purposes of the United Nations.[1]

In 1948, the United Nations Declaration of Human Rights was adopted. Article 26 states,

> Education shall be directed to the full development of the human personality and to the strengthening of respect for human rights and fundamental freedoms. It shall promote understanding, tolerance and friendship among all nations, racial and religious groups, and shall further the activities of the United Nations for the maintenance of peace.[2]

Unfortunately, many nations have violated these requirements and continue to do so. International law prohibits genocide, war

Notes

[1] Carl Mirra, *United States Foreign Policy: and the Prospects for Peace Education* (Jefferson, NC: McFarland & Company Inc., Publishers, 2008), 35.
[2] Carl Mirra, *United States Foreign Policy and the Prospects for Peace Education, 23.*

crimes, and crimes against humanity, but there is no permanent, institutional mechanism to enforce these laws. The International Court of Justice was established in 1945, but it will hear cases between two disputing nations only if the disputing nations agree to submit the issue to the court. Consequently, 160 countries met in Rome in 1998 and formed the International Criminal Court, which is designed to prosecute such offenses.[3] One hundred and twenty-three countries are States Parties to the Rome Statute of the International Criminal Court, including all of the European Union, but the United States has not joined, nor have Russia, China, North Korea, or Iran.[4]

Apparently, the United States, Russia, China, North Korea, and Iran do not want to be prosecuted for actions they take that would be considered war crimes, genocide, or crimes against humanity. The United States does a lot of positive things, and we like to think it is supportive of human rights. On the other hand, the following quotation by Johan Galtung indicates the United States needs to make significant changes in its foreign policies:

> What does so much of the world have against the US Empire? Mainly that it kills, exploits, manipulates, and dictates:
>
> The US Empire has killed 12–16 million in 70 interventions after the Second World War alone to obtain the following three below.
>
> The US Empire, through its hyper-capitalism, brings wealth to some but condemns very many to misery, and kills them through malnutrition, and lack of affordable prevention therapy.
>
> The US Empire manipulates all over, including the United Nations politically, like in John Perkins's *Confessions of an Economic Hit Man.*

---

[3] Carl Mirra, *United States Foreign Policy and the Prospects for Peace Education,* 130.

[4] "Assembly of States Parties to the Rome Statute," International Criminal Court, revised December 13, 2022, asp.icc-cpi.int/states-parties.

> The US Empire thinks it has a God-given monopoly on truth, imposes its own approach, and is today unfit for dialogue.[5]

These words may be excessively offensive, but they indicate a problem with the way the United States relates to some other nations. Some examples would be the Bay of Pigs Invasion of Cuba; the overthrow of Prime Minister Mosaddegh in Iran; the wars in Vietnam, Iraq, and Afghanistan; and the United States' interference in Nicaragua and El Salvador.

If the United States would take seriously the requirements of the United Nations Charter and join the International Criminal Court, this would provide a good example for other nations and significantly reduce a lot of the hostile feelings that result in violence.

The basic concept of laws that are designed democratically and enforced professionally is a good idea that has worked at the local and national levels, and there must be a way to make it work internationally.

The United States has 31 percent of the world's wealth and 4 percent of the world's population. It also has a network of military bases in many different countries.[6] Surely the United States could afford to treat all other countries with the basic courtesy and respect required by the Charter of the United Nations, the United Nations Declaration of Human Rights, and the International Criminal Court. Then the International Criminal Court could help prosecute foreign terrorists who attack the United States.

Currently, the primary international tensions are between democratic and authoritarian forms of government. Democratic governments believe democracy is important and want to encourage other nations to become democratic and protect the human rights of their citizens. On the other hand, democratic governments do not have the power to make other governments change their forms of govern-

---

5   Carl Mirra, United States Foreign Policy and the Prospects for Peace Education, 2.

6   John Paul Lederach and Janice Moomaw Jenner, eds., *A Handbook of International Peacebuilding: Into the eye of the Storm* (San Francisco, CA: Jossey-Bass, 2002).

ment, and they do not have the right to do so. Each nation is entitled to self-government, just as each person is entitled to independence. Perhaps each nation should stop making this an obstacle to friendship with other nations.

History has shown that dictators are eventually replaced. Many authoritarian governments have become democratic, but that needs to be a choice made by the people involved. Individual nations cannot force another nation to change its form or government, but there probably could be a way for the community of nations to restrict any nation from invading another. International law is not yet mature in its development, but gradual progress is being made. At some point, each nation may realize that well-designed international law is to the advantage of all nations.

North Korea has nuclear weapons, and there is no indication that North Korea is likely to give them up. Our sanctions have not been effective in stopping the production of these weapons. Instead, the sanctions have increased their attitude that we are their enemy and that they need to gain more power to make us change our policies. If we stop the sanctions and engage in dialogue with North Korea, we may be able to reverse this hostility.

The United States should also stop trying to put pressure on China to change its internal policies concerning human rights. It is obvious that our pressure is not changing China's policies. There are several authoritarian nations that oppress their citizens and deny their citizens' basic human rights. We are not likely to force them to change, but with time, their citizens may find a way to change them. There may also be private organizations and businesses that can influence such changes. The governments of each nation need to accept one another on a friendly basis and keep diplomatic channels open so differences can be discussed and friendships maintained. This would comply with the United Nations Charter, and it would be up to the United Nations to advocate for the provisions of the Declaration of Human Rights.

With China, there is also the issue of Taiwan. This is a very sensitive issue because China considers Taiwan a part of China. The United States needs to tread lightly and avoid doing things that irritate China concerning Taiwan. We do not want Russia or China interfering with our domestic affairs, and we should not interfere in theirs. On the other hand, there should be some way for the international community to prevent China from invading Taiwan, just as there should have been some way to prevent Russia from invading Ukraine.

If the United States decides to change its international practices, abide by the charter of the United Nations, and join the International Criminal Court, can we expect China, Russia, North Korea, and Iran to do the same? We probably should not expect them to, but these authoritarian countries look at the history of the United States and feel threatened and disrespected. The United States is in the best position to take the first step in the direction of peace, and that eventually will make it more likely for other nations to follow. It will be very important for the United States to avoid doing things that can be seen as a threat to other nations and criticizing other nations. It will also be very important for the United States to arrange a lot of dialogue with each of these other nations and to continue the intensive dialogue for years. The dialogues should be designed with the help and participation of one or more third parties that have extensive experience in international conflict transformation.

The book edited by John Paul Lederach and Janice Moomaw Jenner, entitled *A Handbook of International Peacebuilding: Into the Eye of the Storm*, is an excellent resource for examining the ways a well-trained third party can help resolve conflicts in international settings and the issues to consider before serving as such a third party.[7] There are several ways each of us can help prevent violence internationally. We can encourage our government to avoid acting like a bully in relation to other nations. We can participate in cultural exchange programs in which we develop friendships with people from other nations. We can contribute to humanitarian efforts to improve health and living conditions in other countries where economic opportunities are limited.

---

[7] Lederach and Moomaw Jenner, eds., *A Handbook of International Peacebuilding: Into the Eye of the Storm*.

One example of a family that helped improve international relations was Sam and Miriam Levering, who were apple farmers in Virginia. Tom Hastings, in his book *Nonviolent Response to Terrorism*, says they were Quakers who were active in the Friends Committee on National Legislation. In 1970, the United States drafted a proposed treaty to consolidate and codify the Law of the Sea. United States industries and mining corporations wanted preference given to US-based companies that could use expensive technologies. Sam and Miriam Levering "led the citizen-based coalition of educational groups, peace organizations, environmental groups and other NGOs in a ten-year process and succeeded both nationally and at the international level in creating and preserving most of the positive aspects of the Law of the Sea. Quite literally, without their involvement, it is entirely possible that poorer nations would have much less power, income and claim to the resources that are shared by the world. It is also likely that, without the leadership of a Quaker couple with no expertise at the outset, the environmental protections so important to ocean preservation would have been much weaker."[8]

Another example of local citizens helping to prevent violence was the International Campaign to Ban Landmines. Jody Williams was a nurse from Vermont who had seen a lot of casualties from leftover landmines in Southeast Asia. She coordinated more than one thousand nongovernmental organizations in publicizing the problem and was successful in getting the ban made into international law.[9]

International conflicts will continue to result in violence until more nations seriously implement Article 26 of the United Nations Declaration of Human Rights, as described earlier in this chapter. A lot of schools already have classes in peace education, and a lot of teachers have been trained to teach these classes. Their focus is on presenting facts and promoting discussions and student inquiry, not insisting on the acceptance of a particular point of view. They

---

[8] Tom Hastings, *Nonviolent Response to Terrorism* (Jefferson, NC: McFarland & Company Inc., Publishers, 2004), 77.
[9] Hastings, Nonviolent Response to Terrorism, 78.

do point out both good and bad things that have been done by the United States, but they focus on reconciliation instead of condemning the past.[10]

---

[10] Mirra, United States Foreign Policy and the Prospects for Peace Education, 31–32.

CHAPTER 10

Civil Wars

Civil wars sometimes become more of a problem than wars between nations. Between 1945 and 1999, civil wars killed more than sixteen million people, compared to three million killed by wars between nations.[1] These civil wars can be prevented by the use of nonviolent conflict management or strategic nonviolent rebellion that succeeds twice as often as violent insurrection, and the result will produce more civil rights, human rights, and democracy, and the cost will be much less.[2]

Strategic nonviolence uses "protests, strikes, boycotts, and demonstrations without using or threatening physical harm against the opponent."[3] It also focuses on respect and dignity.

Civil strife frequently results from leaders who rule by fear and violence, leaders who are corrupt, and leaders who are not honest with the people they govern. Frequently, there are conflicts over resources, ethnic or religious divisions, democratic aspirations, or thoughts of secession.

Notes

[1] Tom Hastings, *A New Era of Nonviolence: The Power of Civil Society over War* (Jefferson, NC: McFarland & Company Inc. Publishers, 2014), 15.
[2] Hastings, A New Era of Nonviolence: The Power of Civil Society over War, 79.
[3] Hastings, A New Era of Nonviolence: The Power of Civil Society over War, 84.

Some of the roles that can help prevent civil wars include peace-oriented journalism, training in nonviolent strategies, coalition building, truth and reconciliation processes, and third-party mediation. Mediators must develop the skills needed and gain an understanding of the situation. They need to understand who the stakeholders are and make sure they are involved in the process.

In 1989–1990, nonviolent revolutions occurred in thirteen nations, and all were successful except for China.[4]

Violent action produces victims, and these victims tend to harbor hatred and seek revenge. This can be avoided if violence is not used.

The negotiation process starts with gathering information. Then options are developed. Then the options are evaluated. Then a planning phase is developed and agreed upon. All sides need to be reasonably satisfied. Through this process, new paths that were not obvious earlier can be developed.

---

[4] Tom Hastings, *Nonviolent Response to Terrorism* (Jefferson, NC: McFarland & Company Inc. Publishers, 2004), 86.

CHAPTER 11

—

Defensive Strategies

Defense is an essential part of violence prevention. There will always be people who try to gain wealth, status, or some other advantage by forcibly taking things from other people or by forcing their will on other people. It has been said that a common cause of war is unprotected wealth.

In the United States, we have a system of laws that are developed by local, state, and national governments to protect us from people who might want to use violence against us. Law enforcement officers are responsible for enforcing the laws and protecting the public. This can be an overwhelming responsibility. Any time people are given power and authority to exercise violence, there will be situations in which this power is abused. We need to be sure we have checks and balances to prevent misuse of this authority.

Another important aspect of defense is the military. Each nation has the right to defend itself. On the other hand, some nations use their military to threaten or invade other nations. There should be a way to prevent this. Even the process of testing weapons and conducting military exercises can escalate tensions among nations and stimulate an arms race. North Korea is an example of this. This is not something individual nations can resolve. There needs to be a way for the international community to have defensive capabilities that can protect both large and small nations. For this to work, there must be a way for nations to work together for the common good. There must be some kind of agreement that even the smallest nations will be defended by the international community.

Some people think a nation should build up a huge defensive capability to deter invasion by another country. On the other hand, if we build up a huge military capability, the neighboring country may feel threatened by this and decide to attack. Defense is important, but the establishment of friendship and trust is just as important. It is much better to make a friend than an enemy. Perhaps there can be some kind of international agreement concerning reasonable defensive capabilities. This is especially important in relation to nuclear weapons.

As citizens, we can do things to reduce the probability of being the target of violence. For instance, we can avoid doing or saying things that are likely to antagonize other people. We can also learn how to listen to the concerns of other people and address their concerns in nonviolent ways.

In the United States, there are differing opinions concerning the need for individuals to carry firearms for personal defense. We do have the right to carry firearms if we are old enough and mentally and emotionally capable of handling that responsibility. On the other hand, this nation has more firearms per person than any other nation in the world (120.5 per 100 people compared to Yemen, the next highest, which had 52.8 per 100 people).[1] The United States also has one of the highest rates of firearm-related deaths. Only Jamaica, eight countries in Central and South America, and Eswatini in Africa have higher rates of firearm homicide.[2]

Notes

[1] Global Firearms Holdings-Small Arms Survey, "Estimating Global Civilian-Held Firearms Numbers," updated June 2018, smallarmssurvey.org/sites/default/files/resources/SAS-BP-Civilian-Firearms-Numbers.pdf.
[2] Wikipedia, "List of Countries by Firearm-Related Death Rate," updated November 2011, en.wikipedia.org/Wiki/List_of_countries_by_firearm-related_death_rate.

A study was done in three US cities in 1998 concerning firearms in the home. This study found that "for every time a gun in the home was used in a self-defense or legally justifiable shooting, there were four unintentional shootings, seven criminal assaults, or homicides, and eleven attempted or complete suicides." The conclusion was that "guns kept in the home are more likely to be involved in a fatal or nonfatal accidental shooting, criminal assault, or suicide attempt than to be used to injure or kill in self-defense."[3]

The people who engage in mass shootings seem to choose assault-style weapons because they want to be recognized for killing a huge number of people, and they would be less likely to conduct these shootings if they did not have access to such weapons. At least, the number of people killed in mass shootings would be less if such weapons were not available.

Many schools, public offices, airports, and events that attract huge crowds have adopted policies that prevent people from carrying firearms into those places. This appears to be an effective way to reduce the chance of mass shootings in these settings.

The whole issue concerning firearms has become a political issue with very strong opinions on both sides. This is the kind of issue that requires honest, open discussions from both sides so decisions can be made that respect the needs of both parties. Each of us might have the kind of insight needed to encourage serious bipartisan discussions on this topic. This is another situation in which it would probably be helpful to involve a third party to facilitate such discussions.

---

[3] A. L. Kellerman, "Injuries and Deaths Due to Firearms in the Home," National Library of Medicine, Summary, *J. Trauma*, 45(2):263–7 (August 1998), http://pubmed.ncbi.gov/971518/.

CHAPTER 12

—

Conclusions

Violence is a huge problem in the United States and around the world. It results in a lot of economic costs as well as pain, suffering, and death. A lot of this violence can be prevented. One approach is to reduce the things we do that trigger violence in the people around us. Another approach is to teach children, young people, and parents how to respond to conflict and stressful situations without violence and why it is important to learn these skills.

There are also a lot of changes we can make in our society to reduce stress and enable nations and individuals to resolve their conflicts in nonviolent ways. The most important thing is to recognize conflicts in their early stages and promote open dialogue concerning the issues. Another important thing is to teach children and parents how to resolve problems without violence and to respect all people.

Frequently, it is helpful to involve a third party in resolving conflicts. These changes will take time to implement, and there will be people who will not support them. There will continue to be individuals and national leaders who think violence is the only way to resolve some conflicts. On the other hand, history has shown that conflicts can be resolved peacefully, and teaching the methods of doing that will cost a lot less than the cost of violence.

As you consider all the strategies for preventing violence, you may feel overwhelmed. The task is huge, but it can easily be spread among a large number of people. If each person just chooses one or two parts of the task, progress can be made. Fortunately, these same activities will produce a lot of other benefits for our society. For example, improving parenting skills will improve family tranquility, student performance, and emotional stability. Preventing and treating mental illness will improve the quality of life for people who have problems as well as the people around them, and learning how to resolve conflicts and how to make friends instead of enemies can bring a lot of pleasure into our lives.

If enough nations can agree to the conditions outlined in chapter 9, the world will be a much safer place, and a lot more resources will be available for solving other problems.

BIBLIOGRAPHY

———

"Alternatives to Violence Project." Updated January 21, 2022. AVPUSA.com.

American Psychological Association, Commission on Violence and Youth. "Violence & Youth." Issued 1993. apa.org/pi/prevent-violence/resources/violence-youth.pdf.

American Psychological Association. "What Makes Kids Care? Teaching Gentleness in a Violent World." Created 2013. www.apa.org/topics/parenting/teaching-kids-gentleness.

Bachman, James John. *Why Can't We Talk: Christian Wisdom as a Habit of the Heart.* Woodstock, Vermont: Skylight Paths Publishing, 2013.

Bish, Joseph J., "A Breakdown of the United Nations World Population Prospects 2022 Report." Population Media Center. org. Created July 14, 2022.

Braver Angels. braverangels.org. Accessed January 01, 2023.

Center for Disease Control. "Violence Prevention Home Page." Revised September 28, 2021. cdc.gov/violenceprevention/index.html.

Dudley, Dominic. "Cost of Violence around the World Estimated at $14 Trillion a Year US Facing Biggest Bill." *Forbes.* June 12, 2019. *https://www.forbes.com/sites/dominicdudley/2019/cost-of-violence.*

Du Mont, Rhea, Tom H. Hastings, and Emiko Noma, eds. *Conflict Transformation: Essays on Methods of Nonviolence.* Jefferson, NC: McFarland & Company Inc. Publishers, 2013.

Ferguson, Sarah. "Take Action to Eliminate Female Genital Mutilation Now." UNICEF USA. Created February 5, 2019. unicefusa.org/stories/take-action-eliminate-female-genital- mutilation-now.

Gilligan, James. *Preventing Violence.* New York: Thames and Hudson Inc., 2001.

Global Firearms Holdings-Small Arms Survey. "Estimating Global Civilian-Held Firearms Numbers." June 2018. smallarmssurvey.org/sites/default/files/resources/SAS-BP- Civilian-Firearms-Numbers.pdf.

Gordon, Thomas, *Parent Effectiveness Training: The Proven Program for Raising Responsible Children.* New York, NY: Harmony Publishing, 2019.

Haltiwanger, John. "America's 20-year War on Terra Has Killed up to 929,000 People and Cost over $8 Trillion: Report." *Insider.* August 31, 2021. www.businessinsider.com/us-war-on-terror.

Hastings, Tom. *A New Era of Nonviolence: The Power of Civil Society over War.* Jefferson, NC: McFarland & Company Inc. Publishers, 2014.

Hastings, Tom. *Nonviolent Response to Terrorism.* Jefferson, NC: McFarland & Company Inc. Publishers, 2004.

Heaney, Robert S. Zeyneb Sayilgan, and Claire Haymes. *Faithful Neighbors: Christian-Muslim Visions and Practice.* Harrisburg, Pennsylvania: Morehouse Publishing, 2016.

Huesman, L. Rowell. "The Contagion of Violence: The Extent, the Process, and the Outcome." Institute for Social Research, University of Michigan. Viewed December 30, 2022. ncbi.nlm.nih.gov/books/NBK189992/.

International Criminal Court. "Assembly of States Parties to the Rome Statute." Updated December 13, 2022. asp.icc-cpi.int/states-parties.

Kellerman, A. L. "Injuries and Deaths Due to Firearms in the Home." National Library of Medicine, Summary, *J. Trauma.* 45(2):263–7 (August 1998). http://pubmed.ncbi.nim.nih.gov/971518/.

Lakey, George. *How We Win: A Guide to Nonviolent Direct Action Campaigning.* Brooklyn, NY: Melville House Publishing, 2018.

Lederach, John Paul. *The Little Book of Conflict Transformation: Clear Articulation of the Guiding Principles by a Pioneer in the Field.* New York, NY: Good Books of Skyhorse Publishing Inc., 2003.

Lederach, John Paul, and Janice Moomaw Jenner, eds. *A Handbook of International Peacebuilding: Into the Eye of the Storm.* San Francisco, California: John Wiley & Sons, 2002.

Lederach, John Paul. *Preparing for Peace: Conflict Transformation across Cultures.* Syracuse, NY: Syracuse University Press, 1996.

McCarthy, Colman, ed. *Solutions to Violence.* Washington, DC: Center for Teaching Peace, 2002.

Merrick, J. S. et al. "Benevolent Childhood Experiences (BCE) in Homeless Parents: A Validation and Replication Study." *Journal of Family Psychology.* 33, No.4 (2019).

Mirra, Carl. *United States Foreign Policy and the Prospects for Peace Education.* Jefferson, NC: McFarland & Company Inc. Publishers, 2008.

Nation, Maury et al. "What Works in Prevention Principles of Effective Prevention Programs." NIH National Library of Medicine. Abstract. *Am Psychol.* June–July; 58(6–7):449–56 (2003). doi:10.1037/0003-066x6-7.449. http://pubmed.ncbi. nim.nih-gov/12971191/.

NIH National Library of Medicine. "6 Direct and Indirect Costs of Violence." Viewed December 30, 2022. ncbi.nlm.nih.gov/ books/NBK189992/.

North Carolina DHHS Chronic Disease and Injury Section. Injury and Violence Prevention Branch. Updated December 05, 2022. injuryfreenc.dph.ncdhhs.gov.

Peterson, Jillian, and James Densley. *The Violence Project: How to Stop a Mass Shooting Epidemic.* New York, NY: Abrams Press, 2021.

"Resolution 2198 (XXI) adopted by the United Nations General Assembly." UNHCR. Accessed January 1, 2023. unhcr.org/ en-us/3b66c2aa10.

Ripley, Amanda. *High Conflict: Why We Get Trapped and How We Get Out.* New York, NY: Simon & Shuster, 2021.

Sauls, Scott. *A Gentle Answer: Our "Secret Weapon" in an Age of Us against Them.* Nashville, TN: Nelson Books, 2020.

Shure, Myrna B., PhD. "Preventing Violence the Problem-Solving Way." *Office of Juvenile Justice and Delinquency Prevention.* (April

1999). https://ojjdp.ojp.gov/library/publications/preventing-violence-problem-solving-way.

UNICEF. "What Is Female Genital Mutilation? 7 Questions Answered." Updated March 04, 2019. unicef.org/stories/what-you-need-know-about-female-genital-mutilation.

United Nations General Assembly. "Resolution 2198 (XXI) adopted by the United Nations General Assembly." UNHCR. Accessed January 1, 2023. unhcr.org/en-us/3b66c2aa10.

United Nations Office of Drugs and Crime. "Killing of Women and Girls by Their Intimate Partners or Other Family Members." Updated November 2021. UNodc.org/documents/data-and-analysis/statistics/crime/UN_BriefFem_ 251121.pdf.

Ury, William, *The Third Side: Why We Fight and How We Can Stop.* New York, NY: Penguin Books, 2000.

Wade, Margaret Sutton. *Nurse Peggy's Notes on Newborns: Caring for Your New Baby.* Raleigh, NC: A Place to Copy, 2022.

Watson Institute of International and Public Affairs of Brown University. "Costs of War." September 2021. watson.brown.edu/costs/economic.

Webster-Stratton, T. Taylor. "Nipping Early Risk Factors in the Bud: Preventing Substance Abuse, Delinquency, and Violence in Adolescents through Interventions Targeted at Young Children (0–8 Years)." Abstract. *NIH National Library of Medicine.* Prev. Sci. 2(3): 165 (Sept. 2001). doi:10.1023/a:1011510923900.

Webster, Daniel W. and Jon S. Vernick, eds. *Reducing Gun Violence in America.* Baltimore, MD: The Johns Hopkins University Press, 2013.

Wikipedia. "List of Countries by Firearm-Related Death Rate." Updated November 2011. en.wikipedia.org/Wiki/List_of_countries_by_firearm-related_death_rate.

World Health Organization. "Female Genital Mutilation." Updated January 21, 2002. WHO.int/news-room/fact-sheets/detail/female-genital-mutilation.

World Health Organization. "Violence Against Women." Updated March 9, 2021. WHO.int/news-room/fact-sheet/detail/violence-against-women.

ACKNOWLEDGMENTS

—

I am deeply grateful for the people who have assisted me in writing this book. My wife, Mary Freas, and my daughters, Ellen Freas and Erica Brewer, have read my drafts and recommended very appropriate modifications. Dr. Sandy Marshall also reviewed one of my drafts and recommended several changes based on his professional experience. Deborah Beckel very wisely encouraged me to add more information concerning violence against women and girls and to enrich other sections of my first draft. Gary York pointed out the importance of elaborating on the connection between anger and violence. He also introduced me to Professor Max Carter, who recommended several excellent books, which I used in my research. Members of the Mount Airy Friends Meeting connected me with Colin Saxton and Jack Ciancio, who both gave me valuable advice; and Kathryn Adams, who shared her experiences working with the Alternatives to Violence Project. Chuck Hawkins, Lisa Brewer, Margaret Wade, Susan Marshall, and Jonathan Pucik also reviewed some of my drafts and provided much-needed encouragement.

ABOUT THE AUTHOR

—

John Freas grew up in Walnut Cove, North Carolina, and received his BA degree in chemistry and master's in social work from UNC in Chapel Hill. His entire professional career was focused on helping to solve social problems. He worked in six North Carolina counties, helping low-income and minority neighborhoods find ways to improve resources in their communities. Then he worked in Winston-Salem, North Carolina, in a delinquency prevention program that also provided resettlement services for people returning from prison. Next, he was a social worker with the North Carolina Crippled Children's Program and then a data systems manager for the North Carolina Supplemental Food Program for Women, Infants, and Children.

After retiring in 2002, John volunteered with the Traphill Volunteer Fire Department and Grace Clinic of Yadkin Valley and has been active in Galloway Memorial Episcopal Church. John and his wife, Mary, raised two wonderful daughters, and John raises beef cattle and honeybees on their farm in Wilkes County.

When the United States invaded Afghanistan and Iraq, John started doing research on ways to prevent war and later expanded this to include the prevention of violence in general. He wrote one essay entitled "The Prince of Peace," which was posted on the websites of the Episcopal Peace Fellowship and the Baptist Peace Fellowship. This book, entitled *Violence Prevention: We All Can Help*, is the first book he has written.

Printed in the USA
CPSIA information can be obtained
at www.ICGtesting.com
LVHW091100071123
763047LV00058B/809